SURVIVAL SKILLS

FIRST AID

Cody Crane

Children's Press®
An imprint of Scholastic Inc.

SAFETY NOTE

This book suggests several survival skills techniques. When possible, they should all be done with adult supervision. Observe safety and caution at all times. The author and publisher disclaim all liability for any damage, mishap, injury, illness, or death that may occur from engaging in the survival skills techniques featured in this book or any other use of this book.

Special thanks to our content consultant, Rebecca Petersen, MS, ATC, who is an athletic trainer and the owner of Kinetic LLC, an organization that provides emergency action planning (EAP), CPR/first aid certification, and sport safety education. kineticsportssafety.com

Library of Congress Cataloging-in-Publication Data
Names: Crane, Cody, author. | Francis, Kate, 1976– illustrator.
Title: First aid / by Cody Crane; illustrations by Kate Francis.
Description: First edition. | New York, NY: Children's Press, an imprint of Scholastic Inc., 2023. | Series: A true book: Survival skills | Includes bibliographical references and index. | Audience: Ages 8–10. | Audience: Grades 4–6. | Summary: "A new installment in the A True Book series focusing on Survival Skills"— Provided by publisher.
Identifiers: LCCN 2022022747 (print) | LCCN 2022022748 (ebook) | ISBN 9781338853650 (library binding) | ISBN 9781338853667 (paperback) | ISBN 9781338853674 (ebk)
Subjects: LCSH: First aid in illness and injury—Juvenile literature. | Medical emergencies—Juvenile literature. | Survival—Juvenile literature. | BISAC: JUVENILE NONFICTION / Health & Daily Living / First Aid | JUVENILE NONFICTION / General
Classification: LCC RC86.5 .C73 2023 (print) | LCC RC86.5 (ebook) | DDC 616.02/52—dc23/eng/20220613
LC record available at https://lccn.loc.gov/2022022747
LC ebook record available at https://lccn.loc.gov/2022022748

10 9 8 7 6 5 4 3 2 1   23 24 25 26 27

Printed in China, 62
First edition, 2023

Design by Kathleen Petelinsek
Series produced by Spooky Cheetah Press

Find the Truth!

Everything you are about to read is true *except* for one of the sentences on this page.

Which one is **TRUE**?

T or F   Some plants can cause blisters, burning, and itching on a person's skin.

T or F   A mosquito's sharp teeth make its bite itchy.

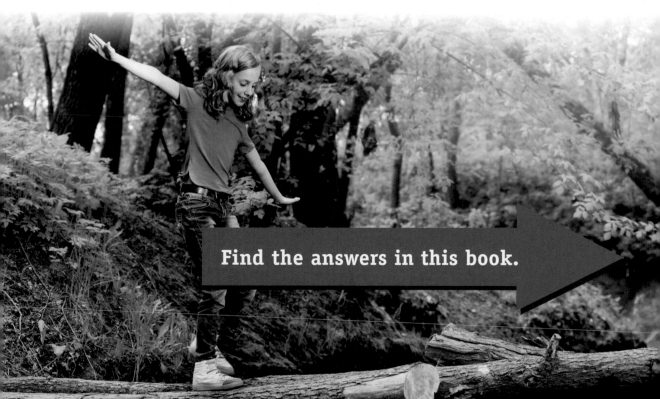

Find the answers in this book.

What's in This Book?

The BIG Truth

Watch out for bees and ticks in summer!

How to Pack a First Aid Kit

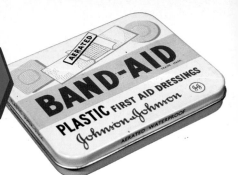

Self-stick bandages were invented in 1920.

Minor injuries can be treated with first aid.

Be Prepared!

Picture this: You are hiking with a group of kids and adults up a steep hill. Suddenly, someone trips and **skins their knee**. If you know first aid, you will know what to do. First aid is immediate care given to a person who is sick or injured. Many types of **medical emergencies** can occur on outdoor adventures—even when people are being careful! You can **help by following the three Cs**. First, **CHECK** for danger. Make sure helping will not put you in harm's way. Second, if the emergency is serious, **CALL 911**. First aid will help you manage some injuries on your own. But when a person's life is at risk, always call for help. Third, if necessary, provide medical **CARE** until professionals arrive.

In 1870, a military doctor came up with the phrase "first aid" to describe treatment given to injured soldiers on the battlefield.

Make sure someone in your group has first aid supplies to treat injuries during a hike (see page 26).

Covering a cut can help it heal better.

A scrape caused by sliding against the ground is sometimes called "road rash."

1

Scrapes and Cuts

Scrapes and cuts are some of the most common types of outdoor injuries. Usually, these wounds are small. They just break the surface of the skin and stop bleeding on their own. Minor scrapes and cuts are simple to care for. But sometimes, these wounds are deep or large. They can be very dangerous if they do not stop bleeding. Being able to treat severe injuries could save a person's life.

Scrapes

Health-care providers call a scrape an **abrasion**. This type of wound happens when skin gets scraped away after rubbing against a rough surface. Abrasions are most likely to happen on a person's elbows, knees, palms, or shins. They can be treated with basic first aid.

Falling off a bike can easily result in a cut or scrape. Wearing knee and elbow pads can offer protection.

HOW TO TREAT A SCRAPE

1 Wash your hands or apply hand sanitizer. Put on gloves if available.

2 Clean the wound gently by rinsing with water if available. Or wipe the area with an **antiseptic** wipe. This gets rid of dirt and debris.

3 If the wound is bleeding, use gauze or a clean cloth to apply pressure. This helps stop any bleeding, usually within a few minutes.

4 Apply a thin layer of antibiotic ointment. This prevents germs from causing an **infection**.

5 Cover the wound with a bandage, especially if it is in a spot that may get dirty.

6 Remove the gloves if you were using them. Wash your hands again or apply hand sanitizer after caring for the wound.

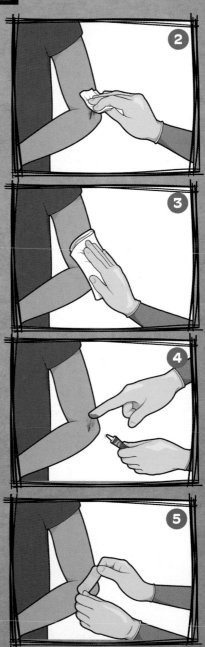

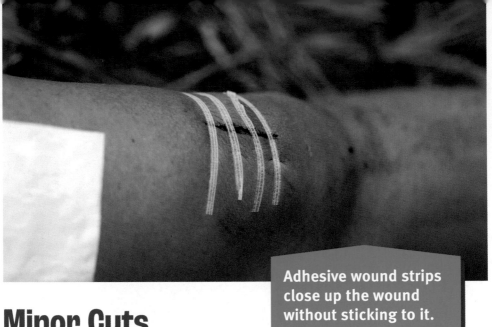

Adhesive wound strips close up the wound without sticking to it.

Minor Cuts

Cuts occur when a sharp object pierces a person's skin. Minor cuts are small—no longer or deeper than the width of your pinkie finger. To treat a minor cut, follow the same steps as for treating a scrape (page 11). Instead of applying a bandage to the cut, you can apply an adhesive wound-closure strip. Stick the strip to the skin on one side of the wound. Pull the strip taut and stick to the other side. This will close the cut. That helps keep out germs, allows for faster healing, and prevents scarring.

An Idea That Stuck

In 1921, the medical supply company Johnson & Johnson introduced a new product. It was the Band-Aid, which had been invented by a company worker the previous year. At first, few people bought the self-stick bandages. Then the company came up with a clever marketing idea. It began adding Band-Aids to first aid kits given to every Boy Scout. The kits became an important part of a Scout's gear. With the help of kids, families became aware of the handy new item.

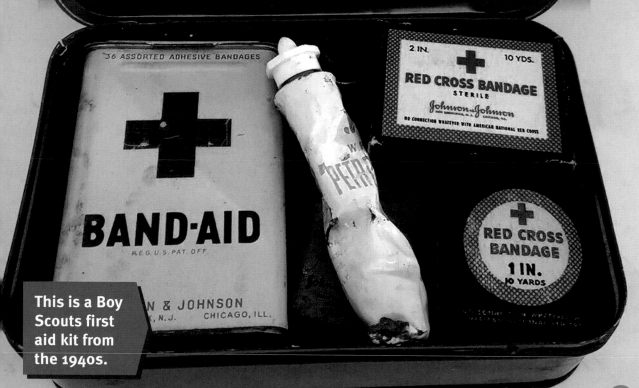

This is a Boy Scouts first aid kit from the 1940s.

Serious Wounds

Some wounds require urgent medical treatment. For example, large, ragged, or deep cuts may require a health-care provider to close the wound with stitches or staples. To control bleeding, use gauze, a T-shirt, or a bandanna to apply continuous direct pressure to the wound. If blood soaks through, add another layer of material to the area. **Call 911 for immediate medical help if the bleeding does not stop.** Bleeding through at least two layers of dressing can be life threatening. Heavy bleeding that spurts or does not stop may need a tourniquet. Tourniquets should ONLY be applied to a limb (arm or leg).

A tourniquet slows the flow of blood. It can potentially save someone's life in the event of a severe injury.

HOW TO APPLY A TOURNIQUET

1 Place a long strip of cloth 2 to 3 inches (5 to 8 centimeters) above the wound. Do not place it directly on the wound.

2 Cross the ends of the cloth over the limb. Place a short stick or similar-shaped sturdy object (like a spoon) where the cloth overlaps.

3 Tie a knot to secure the stick to the cloth. Twist the stick to tighten the cloth until blood stops flowing from the wound.

4 Use a small strip of cloth wrapped around the limb to tie one end of the stick in place so it cannot unwind.

5 Write down the time the tourniquet was applied. You will need to share this information with a health-care provider when the time comes.

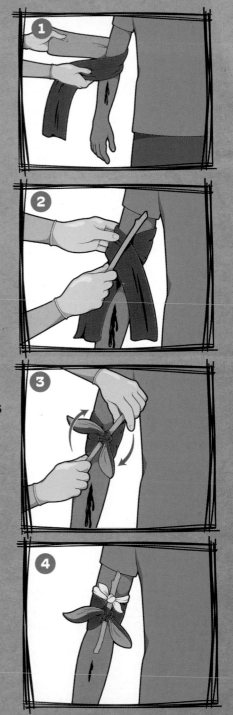

An adult should always supervise a campfire.

If a person's clothing catches fire, they should STOP moving, DROP to the ground, and ROLL to put out the flames.

Burns and Rashes

One of the best parts of any campout is roasting marshmallows around a fire. But get too close to the flames and you could get burned. And fires are not the only thing that can harm your skin when outdoors. Touching certain poisonous plants can result in a painful rash covered in itchy blisters. Being aware of these dangers can help you avoid injuries. But you should also know what to do if someone gets a burn or rash.

How Bad Is the Burn?

Burns are wounds caused by heat, chemicals, radiation, or electricity. They may appear red, white, brown, or black. Burns may also blister, appear swollen, or both. The severity of a burn can range from minor to life threatening. A severe burn can extend through deeper layers of skin, fat, muscle, or bone. **A burn that covers an entire body part and/or affects breathing requires immediate medical attention. In the U.S., call 911!** Minor burns can be treated with basic first aid.

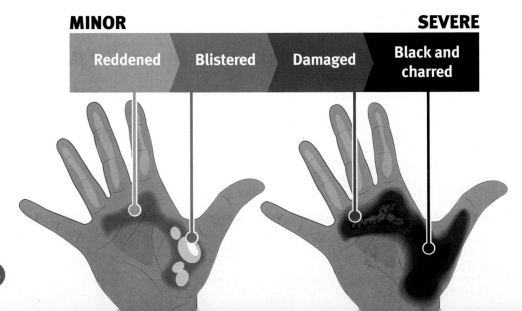

MINOR			SEVERE
Reddened	Blistered	Damaged	Black and charred

HOW TO TREAT A MINOR BURN

1 Remove the affected area from the heat source.

2 Cool the burn by placing it under clean, cool running water as soon as possible for at least 10 to 20 minutes.

3 If running water is not available, you can pour on any cool water on hand or apply a cold compress. You should never use ice or an ice pack.

4 Leave the burn uncovered. Do not apply any ointment to the wound—it could cause an infection.

5 If the burn has caused blistering, it should be examined by a health-care provider. You can cover the burn loosely with a sterile dressing if it will take longer than 10 minutes to reach care.

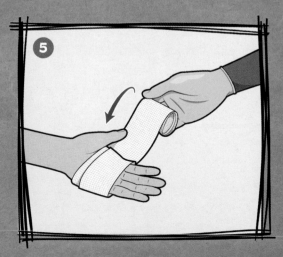

Poisonous Plants

Certain plants are poisonous. It is good to know what they look like so you can avoid touching them. Poison ivy, poison oak, and poison sumac have leaves coated with sticky toxic oil. Even slight contact can cause an itchy, blistering rash. Stinging nettle is covered in tiny needle-like hairs.

Poison ivy

Poison oak

Poison sumac

Timeline: History of First Aid

1862
The first ambulance corps is set up in the United States.

1863
The Red Cross, an aid organization that helps in times of crisis, is founded.

1888
Johnson & Johnson creates the first aid kit.

1921
Johnson & Johnson introduces the first self-stick bandages, branded BAND-AID.

These hairs inject chemicals into your skin, also causing blisters, burning, and itching. To treat any of these rashes, wash the area with soap and water to remove the plant's oil or hairs. Then apply calamine lotion or hydrocortisone cream to relieve itching. **Call 911 if the person shows signs of a severe allergic reaction, such as swelling or difficulty breathing.**

Stinging nettle

If you swallow something poisonous, call the Poison Control Hotline: 1-800-222-1222 in the U.S.

1960
Cardiopulmonary resuscitation (CPR) to assist people whose hearts have stopped beating is invented.

1968
In the United States, 911 is established for emergency calls.

1974
Dr. Henry Heimlich introduces abdominal thrusts to treat choking.

Only female mosquitoes bite.

Mosquitoes are most active at dawn and dusk.

Bites and Stings

Biting and stinging insects can ruin a fun day outdoors. But there are ways to keep these pesky bugs at bay. For example, wear long pants and sleeves and apply insect repellent to any uncovered parts to prevent mosquitoes from biting. When a mosquito bites, it injects **saliva** into your skin. Your body reacts to the substance by producing an itchy, red bump. Apply antihistamine or hydrocortisone cream to relieve itching. Or you can spread on a paste made of baking soda and water. And do not scratch! That could cause the bite to become infected.

Bees and Wasps

Bees and wasps have stingers that inject **venom** into a person's skin. The venom causes pain and slight swelling. Luckily, stings can be treated with first aid. **Call 911 if the person shows signs of a severe allergic reaction, such as swelling or difficulty breathing.**

Bee

Wasp

HOW TO TREAT AN INSECT STING

1. Remove the stinger by scraping it away with your fingernail or some gauze. Avoid using tweezers, as that may cause more venom to be released.

2. Wash the area with soap and water to clean the sting.

3. Place a cold cloth or cold pack on the area for about 10 minutes to reduce pain and swelling. Repeat as necessary.

4. Apply antihistamine or hydrocortisone cream, or a paste made of baking soda and water. All of these can relieve itching.

After removing the tick, keep it in a small plastic bag to show a doctor in case Lyme disease symptoms appear.

Ticks

If a tick gets on your body, it can **burrow** into your skin to drink blood. Some ticks carry bacteria that cause **Lyme disease**. The disease is passed to humans through the bite of an infected tick. Ticks must be removed right away. Use tweezers to grasp the tick close to the surface of your skin to pull out its entire body. Clean the bite area with soap and water. The person should see a doctor if a fever or bull's-eye rash around the bite develops. Those could be signs of Lyme disease.

How to Pack a First Aid Kit

A first aid kit is essential to treating outdoor injuries. You could buy a kit from a store, but it is simple enough to make your own. Here are some of the items you should include. Keep your kit where you can access it easily in your backpack, car, or home.

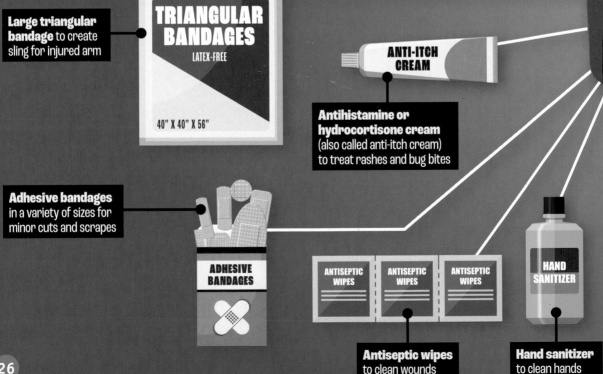

Large triangular bandage to create sling for injured arm

TRIANGULAR BANDAGES
LATEX-FREE
40" X 40" X 56"

ANTI-ITCH CREAM

Antihistamine or hydrocortisone cream (also called anti-itch cream) to treat rashes and bug bites

Adhesive bandages in a variety of sizes for minor cuts and scrapes

ADHESIVE BANDAGES

ANTISEPTIC WIPES   **ANTISEPTIC WIPES**   **ANTISEPTIC WIPES**

HAND SANITIZER

Antiseptic wipes to clean wounds

Hand sanitizer to clean hands

Nitrile or vinyl gloves to wear when caring for open wounds

Medical tape to hold gauze or bandages in place, and to treat a sprained finger or toe

Compression bandage to wrap injured ankles or wrists

INSTANT COLD PACK

Instant cold pack to treat swelling

FIRST AID KIT

Scissors to cut cloth, gauze, tape, or bandages

Tweezers to remove splinters or ticks

ANTIBIOTIC OINTMENT

Antibiotic ointment to prevent infection and help wounds heal quickly

EMERGENCY BLANKET

STERILE PAD

Sterile gauze pads to stop bleeding

Emergency blanket to keep injured person warm

The three most common spots for sprains are ankles, knees, and wrists.

Falls are the most common cause of injury for children of any age.

Sprains and Breaks

Running, climbing, and hiking are fun, but they can sometimes lead to injury. The most common is bruising. More serious injuries include a **sprained** ankle or wrist, which is when the tissue that connects the bones is injured; a fractured (or broken) bone; or a dislocation, which is when a **joint** is out of its normal position. Fractures and dislocations require immediate medical attention.

Check the Injury

If a person falls and injures an arm or a leg, find a safe place for them to sit. Check for broken bones bulging under or poking through the skin. **If it is obvious a bone is out of place or if the pain is severe, call 911 immediately. Let the person rest; do not try to provide first aid.** If the injury is swollen, bruised, or tender, the person may have a sprain. That can be treated with first aid.

HOW TO TREAT A SPRAINED ANKLE

1 Rest the leg in a raised position, above the heart if possible. Apply a cold pack to the injured area for 20 minutes. Both will help with swelling and pain.

2 Support the ankle by wrapping it in a compression bandage. Hold the end of the bandage against the sole of the foot near the toes. Wrap the bandage around the foot moving toward the ankle with each pass. The wrap should be snug but not so tight it cuts off **circulation** to the foot. The person's toes should not look pale or blue in color.

3 Stretch the bandage over the top of the foot and under to form a figure-eight pattern.

4 Continue wrapping the injury, moving up the leg. Use an overlapping method and figure-eight pattern around the ankle until you reach the end of the bandage.

5 Secure the end of the bandage with clips or medical tape.

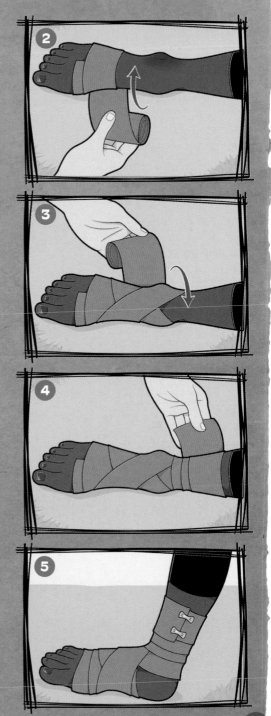

It is important to keep an injured limb from moving.

Sprained Wrists, Fingers, and Toes

For a sprained wrist, finger, or toe, use a splint to keep the injured body part from moving.

Wrist: Place a piece of cardboard or other stiff material beneath the injured arm. It should extend from the palm to the elbow. Wrap a compression bandage around the arm and cardboard. Start at the hand and work your way to the elbow. Secure the bandage in place.

Fingers and Toes: Place a sprained finger on top of a tongue depressor, stick, or spoon and secure it with medical tape. Tape an injured toe to the one next to it to keep it from moving.

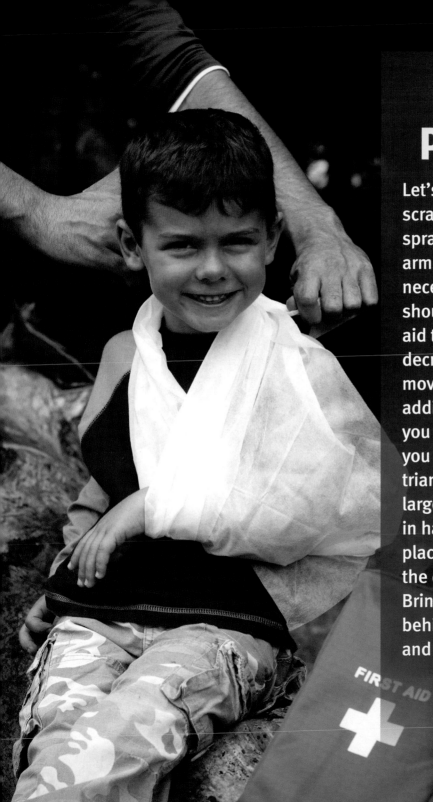

Added Protection

Let's say a person has scraped, cut, burned, or sprained some part of their arm. While not always necessary, you can add a shoulder sling to your first aid treatment. This can help decrease pain by limiting movement and providing additional support. If you don't have a sling, you can make one from a triangular bandage or a large square cloth folded in half diagonally. Then place the person's elbow at the center of the triangle. Bring the ends of the cloth behind the person's neck and tie them together.

The best way to stay safe around water is to learn to swim!

Always swim with a buddy so you can help each other in case of trouble.

Breathing Trouble

A person can stop breathing for a variety of reasons. They may be drowning and water has gotten into their lungs. Or they might be choking on food or an object they have swallowed. A person can stop breathing if they suffer a heart attack, too. This happens when blood flow to the heart is blocked. A person could die in as little as eight minutes without oxygen, so quick action is required!

In Case of Choking

Someone may signal they are choking by clutching their hand to their throat. If they cannot breathe, cough, or speak, perform back blows and **abdominal** thrusts (also known as the Heimlich maneuver).

If a person is coughing or talking, they are not choking. Do not perform first aid. Encourage the person to keep coughing.

HOW TO CARE FOR A CHOKING PERSON

1 Confirm the person is choking and ask if you can help.

2 To perform back blows, support the victim with one arm while striking firmly against the person's back five times with the heel of your other hand.

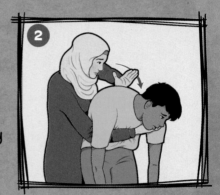

3 To perform abdominal thrusts, place your fist thumb-side-in above the person's belly button (a). Cover your fist with your other hand and give five inward and upward thrusts (b).

4 Continue steps 2 and 3 until the object comes out or the person is able to cough or speak.

5 If the victim is obviously pregnant or too large for abdominal thrusts, place your hand on the center of the chest and give inward and upward thrusts.

⚠️ **WARNING**

If you babysit infants, you should get specific training in how to administer back blows and abdominal thrusts to babies.

Air Assistance

If a person stops breathing for any reason other than choking, **call 911 immediately!** Cardiopulmonary resuscitation (CPR) helps to circulate blood and oxygen to the body until help arrives. It can save someone's life! To perform CPR properly, it is best to take a course and become certified (ages 9 and up).

HOW TO GIVE HANDS-ONLY CPR TO ADULTS AND CHILDREN

1 Lay the person on their back. Kneel next to the person's chest.

2 Place the heel of your hand in the center of the person's chest, with your fingers pointed toward their other side. Place your other hand on top of the first, with your fingers pointed in the same direction. Lace your fingers together.

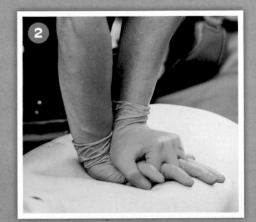

If an emergency arises, you can still provide care within your level of training. After you have **called 911**, hands-only CPR can be performed until EMS arrives.

You have now learned the basics of first aid. There is just one last tip to remember: in case of emergency, always be quick . . . but keep calm!

3 Place your shoulders over your hands and keep your arms stiff and straight. Push down fast and hard. Allow the chest to move back up. Repeat until help arrives or the person begins breathing on their own.

⚠ **WARNING**

If you care for babies, you should get specific training in CPR for babies. The procedure is the same as for adults and children, using just your index and middle fingers instead of hands and not pushing down as hard.

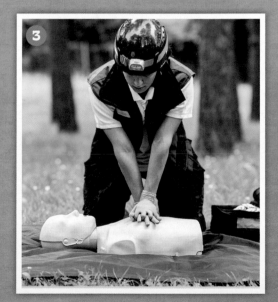

FIRST AID HERO

Davyon was named an honorary deputy for the county sheriff's office in Muskogee, Oklahoma.

When 11-year-old Davyon Johnson saw another student at his school choking, he jumped into action. The student had opened a water bottle with his mouth. The cap had slipped down his throat and gotten stuck. Davyon wrapped his arms around the boy's waist and delivered abdominal thrusts. On Davyon's third squeeze, the cap flew out.

The same day Davyon helped his choking classmate, he saved another life. On the way home from school, he saw smoke coming from a house. People were fleeing the building. But one elderly woman with a walker needed help. Davyon rushed to her aid and led her to safety. For his actions, Davyon was awarded a certificate from the police department in his hometown of Muskogee, Oklahoma.

Davyon was inspired by his uncle to learn first aid.

His uncle is an emergency medical technician. Davyon wants to follow in his footsteps. And even though Davyon is just a kid, he is already well on his way toward that goal. What a hero!

Davyon was honored by Muskogee public schools, the police department, and the county sheriff's office.

Use what you learned in this book to answer the questions below.

1 Which tool from a first aid kit would you use to reduce swelling?

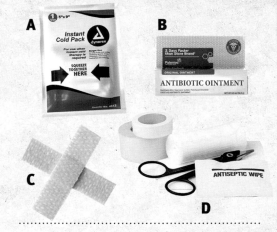

A — Instant Cold Pack

B — ANTIBIOTIC OINTMENT

C

D

ANTISEPTIC WIPE

2 What is the first thing to do when treating a scrape?

A. Clean the wound.

B. Wash your hands.

C. Apply a bandage.

D. Apply antibiotic ointment.

3 If a person's arm or leg is bleeding heavily with no signs of stopping, you should _____.

A. apply pressure

B. apply a tourniquet

C. raise the injured limb

D. do nothing

4 Which type of burn(s) should be treated with first aid? (Choose all that apply.)

A. Severe

B. Minor

C. All

5 Which of the following can carry Lyme disease?

 **A** Mosquito

 **B** Wasp

 **C** Tick

6 Wrapping a sprained ankle will help _____.

A. reduce swelling

B. reduce pain

C. support the injury

D. all of the above

7 Which object would NOT be a good choice to use to make a splint?

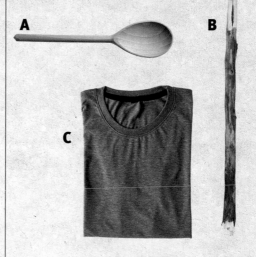

A   **B**   **C**

8 If a person stops breathing for any reason other than choking, what should you do first?

A. Call 911.

B. Check for an object in their mouth.

C. Begin CPR.

D. Rub their back.

True Statistics

Number of people worldwide each year who get trained in CPR and first aid by the American Red Cross: More than 5 million

Percentage of Americans who own a first aid kit: 56%

Number of emergency calls made to 911 each day in the United States: 660,000

Average time it takes for emergency medical service to respond to a 911 call: 8 to 12 minutes

Number of visits that are made to emergency rooms for injuries each year in the United States: 38 million

Did you find the truth?

T Some plants can cause blisters, burning, and itching on a person's skin.

F A mosquito's sharp teeth make its bite itchy.

Resources

Other books in this series:

You can also look at:

Gale, Karen Buhler. *The Kids' Guide to First Aid*. Nashville: WorthyKids, 2000.

Lipman, Grant S. *The Scouting Guide to Wilderness First Aid*. New York: Skyhorse, 2019.

Long, Denise. *Survivor Kid: A Practical Guide to Wilderness Survival*. Chicago: Chicago Review Press, 2011.

Longenecker, Steve. *Steve Longenecker's Wilderness Emergency Medical Aid Book for Kids (and Their Adults)*. Almond, NC: Milestone Press, 2005.

Glossary

abdominal (ab-DAH-muh-nuhl) refers to the part of the body below the chest and above the hips

abrasion (uh-BRAY-zhun) an area of skin that is scraped or rubbed away

antiseptic (an-ti-SEP-tik) a substance that prevents infection by stopping the growth of germs

burrow (BUR-oh) to dig a hole

circulation (sur-kyuh-LAY-shuhn) the movement of blood in blood vessels through the body

infection (in-FEK-shuhn) an illness caused by bacteria or viruses

joint (JOINT) a connection between two bones of a skeleton

Lyme disease (LIME di-zeez) a bacterial disease transmitted by the bite of a tick; if not treated early, the disease can lead to joint pain and heart and nerve problems

saliva (suh-LYE-vuh) a watery mixture produced by an animal's mouth

sprained (SPRAYND) connective tissue in a joint that has been stretched or torn

venom (VEN-uhm) a toxic substance made by some animals that bite or sting, like bees, wasps, spiders, and snakes

Index

Page numbers in **bold** indicate illustrations.

About the Author

Cody Crane is an award-winning nonfiction children's writer. From a young age, she was set on becoming a scientist. She later discovered that writing about science could be just as fun as the real thing. She lives in Houston, Texas, with her husband and son.